A Shark at the Pool

by Sascha Goddard

illustrated by Gareth Conway

OXFORD
UNIVERSITY PRESS

It was a hot morning.
Nan took Max to the pool.

Ben is in the car park!

They all met at the pool.

Max got in the pool.
It was deep.

Look at
me, Nan!

Nan had a turn.
She got in the pool, too.

Nan took off.
She was quick.

Max got hoops for them.

Are you a rocket, Max?

Nan shot up in the hoop.
She was a rocket, too.

Max shot up to hurl the fish.

zoom

Then Max got a shock.

Is it a fin?